ANIMAL TRACKS AND TRACES

ANIMAL TRACKS AND TRACES

BY KATHLEEN V. KUDLINSKI
ILLUSTRATED BY MARY MORGAN

FRANKLIN WATTS
NEW YORK LONDON TORONTO SYDNEY
1991

FOR HAL
ALREADY EXPERT AT TRACKING
OPOSSUMS, GHOST CRABS,
MOOSE . . . AND DRAGONS

K. V. K.

FOR MICHAEL

M.M.

Library of Congress Cataloging-in-Publication Data
Kudlinsky, Kathleen V.
Animal tracks and traces / by Kathleen V. Kudlinski.
p.   cm.
Bibliography: p.
Includes index.
Summary: Discusses the tracks, scents, nests, food remains, and
other traces left by various animals and the clues thus provided
regarding their behavior.
ISBN 0-531-15185-9   ISBN 0-531-10742-6 (lib. bdg.)
1. Animal tracks—Juvenile literature.   2. Animal behavior—
Juvenile literature.   [1. Animal tracks.   2. Animals—Habits and
behavior.]   I. Title.   II. Series.
QL768.K83   1991
591—dc19
88-34546   CIP   AC

CONTENTS

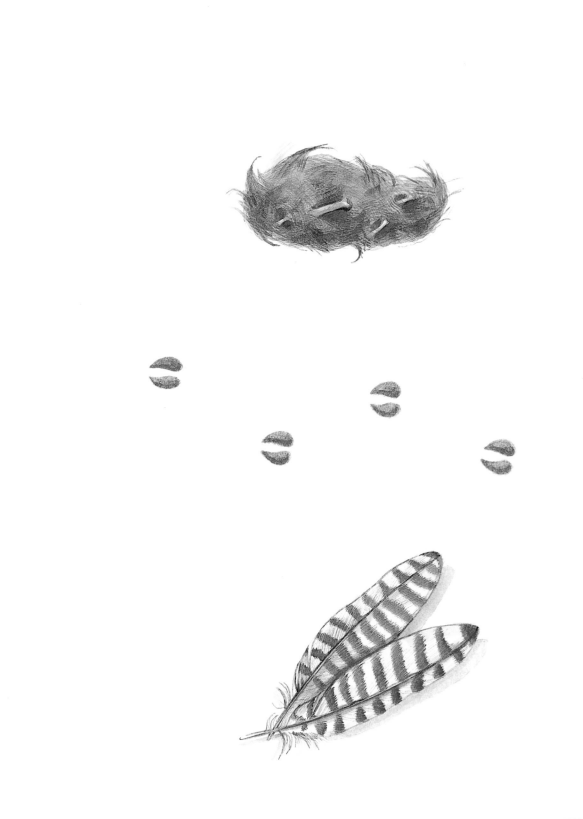

CLUES

"Will you *please* clean up this mess?"

How many times have you heard that? Did you ever wonder how your folks always know whom to blame?

You are probably pretty sloppy about leaving clues behind. Who else would leave:

handprints like yours on the refrigerator?
your favorite cereal on the counter?
your dirty clothes on the floor?
a world-class mess in your own room?

Your folks know whom to blame because they find the clues you leave behind and they know how to read them.

Animals are pretty sloppy about leaving clues behind, too. If you know where to look, you can find their handprints, dirty dishes, old clothing, and messy rooms. Can you tell which animals left these traces on the opposite page?

To see if you were right, look in the back of the book. The answers to all of the tracking puzzles start on page 44.

It's easy to watch how cats, dogs, or other pets behave, but wild animals are shy. They hide so well that most people never even know they are around. You can find out about them from the clues they leave behind. And you can get to see them, too. This book will show you how.

TRACKS

Your dirty handprints or muddy footprints can give you away. Animals leave hand- and footprint clues, too. They leave prints if their paws are dirty. They leave tracks if they step on something soft. Each kind of animal makes a different kind of track.

Can you guess from these clues who was here?

Remember to check your answers at the back of the book.

To read tracks, you need to know how animals' feet are shaped, and how they walk and move.

Furry animals make three different kinds of tracks because of how they walk. Horses and deer walk on the very tips of their toes, like ballerinas. Instead of toenails, these animals have hooves. Their tracks are hoof marks. Horses' hooves leave one mark, shaped like the letter U. Deer and cows have two hooves on each foot.

Cats' and dogs' legs are made so that they walk on their "tippy toes." There is never a heel mark in their tracks. Dog and cat prints seem almost alike, but if you look closely, you can tell them apart. In a dog's track there are tiny marks in front of each toe. These are made by the dog's claws. Cats hold their claws up when they walk. That way, their claws stay sharp and make no mark in a track.

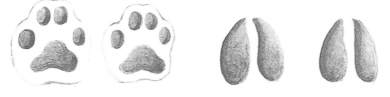

CAT   DEER

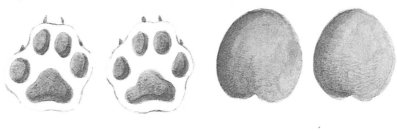

DOG   HORSE

Opossums and raccoons walk on flat feet, like we do. Their front paws leave tracks that look like tiny handprints. Their back paws look like our feet, but with extra-long toes. Both animals are about the same size. How can you tell their tracks apart? Opossums walk with their thumbs and chubby fingers spread wide. Raccoons walk with their skinny fingers and thumbs held closer together. Can you tell these apart?

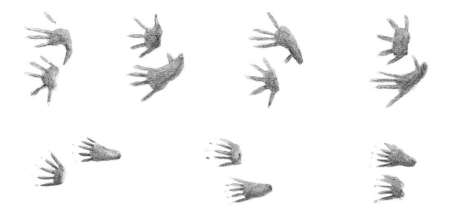

Some furry animals leave tracks of almost the same shape, but they are different sizes. Bigger animals have bigger feet. Which animal made which track?

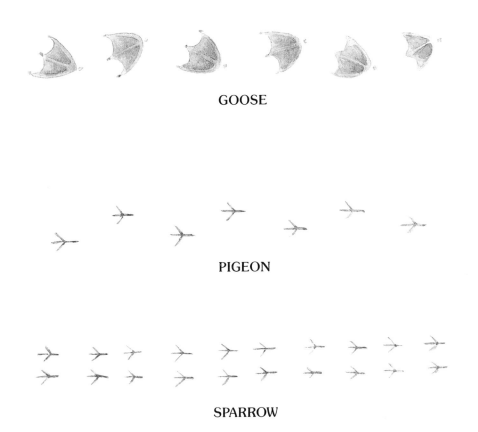

GOOSE

PIGEON

SPARROW

Bird tracks all look alike at first, too. You can tell about where a bird lives by looking at its tracks. Birds that live in the water leave tracks with web marks between the toes. Ducks and geese leave this kind of track.

Birds that spend a lot of time on the ground walk the way we do, moving one foot at a time. Pigeons and starlings are walkers, and make tracks one after another.

Other birds spend most of their time hopping from branch to branch in treetops. They don't know how to walk. When they land on the ground, they hop, making tracks in neat pairs. Sparrows and finches are hopping birds.

HOW TO SET UP A TRACK TRAP

You can find tracks in snow, mud, or sand. Look for them along the muddy sides of creeks or in puddles that have almost dried up.

When you can't find tracks, try making a "track trap." Dig up some dirt or sand until it is soft. Brush it with your hand until it is smooth and flat. Or make a trap indoors by sprinkling flour on a smooth floor. (Remember, *you* have to sweep it up in the morning!) Set some tasty bait in the middle of the trap. Animals will leave tracks in the soft dirt on their way to eat the bait. Many animals will come for peanut butter. Others like sunflower seeds or a bit of meat. Check every morning to see what tracks were made in the night.

SHEDDINGS

If the dirty clothes on the floor are yours, it's easy to guess that you were the one who dropped them there.

Animals leave things behind, too. These are the easiest wildlife clues to read. Only a snake can shed a snake skin. All feathers come from birds. Can you guess who left behind these "dirty clothes"?

Many animals shed their fur. Sometimes you can find wild animal hairs in old birds' nests or lining rabbits' nests in the grass. It is hard to see a hair outdoors. Indoors it is easy to find pet dog or cat fur gathered under sofas or on soft chairs.

Feathers are much easier to find than hairs. Every bird has hundreds of feathers that it sheds at least once a year. In North America, shedding time is late summer, after baby birds have grown. Only a few feathers drop out at a time and new ones grow back quickly. That way birds always have enough feathers to fly away from danger.

If you find a feather, its color and pattern can tell you what kind of bird it came from. The feather's shape can tell you where it grew on the bird. Tiny, fuzzy "down" feathers are a bird's warm undershirt. These feathers don't seem to have any stem, or "shaft," up the middle.

Body feathers cover the down. These feathers are small, but do have shafts. Wing and tail feathers are longer and stiffer. If the shaft goes right down the middle of the feather, it came from a bird's tail. If it is closer to one edge, it came from a wing.

DOWN   BODY   TAIL   WING

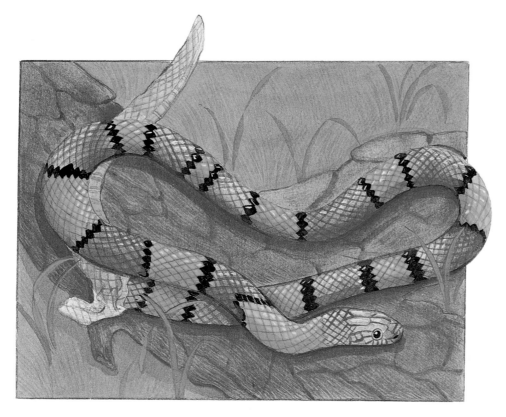

KING SNAKE

Skins that snakes have shed make good collections, too. Snakes shed whenever they have grown too big for their skins. You can find skins any time of year that snakes are awake. A snake starts shedding its skin by rubbing its lips against rough ground or rocks. The skin peels off inside out, like a sock pulled off your foot. New, fresh skin and scales are ready underneath, so the snake just leaves its old skin behind.

Insects and spiders shed their skins, too. Like snakes, their old skins get too tight as they grow. When a new skin is ready underneath, the old skin splits down the back. The insect or spider pulls itself out through the hole. The shed skins keep the shape of the animal, with every leg and hair in place. Mice like to eat these sheddings, so you don't often see this animal clue.

HOW TO COLLECT FEATHERS

Late summer is a good time to make a feather collection. Try to find each kind of feather from a blue jay or pigeon. If they have pulled apart, you can fix them again. Push the broken parts together gently. Then rub softly from the shaft to the feather's edge. Tape them to a piece of paper to make a display for your classroom.

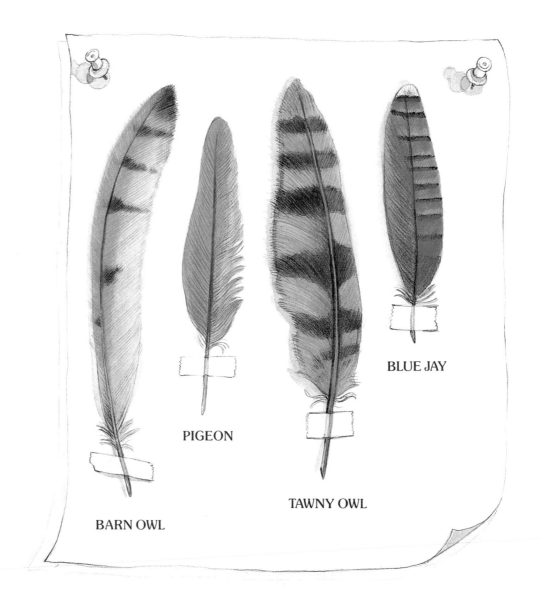

PIGEON

BLUE JAY

TAWNY OWL

BARN OWL

HOW TO SAVE A SNAKESKIN

If you find a snake's shed skin it may be too dry to unfold
without cracking apart. Put it into a jar with a damp paper
towel for a few hours or overnight. When it is soft, gently
pull it out straight. Now you can see all of its scales—even
the two that covered its eyes! You may see shadow marks
where the snake had stripes or spots. If you want to save
the skin, use scissors to cut down the middle of its wide
belly scales. Press it flat and glue it to a piece of cardboard.

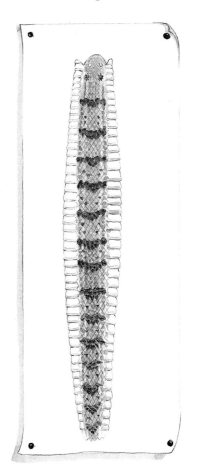

Sheddings are easy to know and fun to collect. The
next animal trace can't be seen or collected.

SCENTS

What is this cat doing? Most people think she is asking to be petted.

She is really rubbing a smell from her chin onto the table leg. This scent is like a sign that tells any other cat that this is her house and her child.

Cats also have scented places on their toes. When they seem to be sharpening their claws, they may be using them to poke their own scent into tree bark—or into a sofa arm.

Rabbits and deer have special smelly places on their bodies, like the cat. They use these to show other deer and rabbits where they have been.

Many animals make signs with their urine.

A male dog lifts his leg to splash his scent high in the air. Other dogs who sniff this signpost can tell whether a male or female dog has been there. They can even tell what kind of a mood the other dog was in! Watch a dog as it walks down a street. It will stop to read scent signs everywhere. And it will probably leave messages of its own for other dogs to read.

Male cats back up to plants or posts to spray their urine. Deer, foxes, and even mice leave this kind of sign.

People can't read the stories "written" in animal scents. Their noses just aren't good enough. But a few animals have smells that are so strong that even *we* can tell them apart. An attic where bats live has a sweet smell. A cat box smells like strong window cleaner. Mice smell worse than rats. And everyone has heard about the smell of a skunk. All skunks have a strong odor. In a pet store, you can sniff this scent by the ferret cage.

You can't smell as well as most mammals, but birds are even worse. They can't smell at all. That is why owls can kill and eat skunks and not mind the stink. And that is why birds do not make scent signs.

All animals have a special scent. Some of it (like a cat's chin scent) you can't smell. Some of it you wish you couldn't smell. But all of it is normal for animals. Knowing about it helps you understand more about the world of animals.

HOW WELL CAN YOU SMELL?

Can you sniff the sharp scent of angry ants when you lift up the rock that covers their nest? Can you smell the ugly, moldy scent that a frightened millipede makes? Can you tell the people in your family apart just by the smell of their skins? Some people can. Others can't.

DIRTY DISHES

Breakfast dishes on the table could have been left by anyone. But if there are pieces of *your* favorite cereal still sticking inside your *own* bowl, the clues point to you.

    An animal left this clue behind when it finished eating. Which of these animals ate here?

It takes practice to see where animals have been nibbling. There are many, many plant eaters. With every bite they take, they leave a clue behind that you can read. House mice and deer mice leave piles of seed coats. Field mice leave neat little piles of grass stems, all cut to the same length. To get to the seeds far over their heads, the mice stand up as tall as they can. They chew through the grass stem. The grass slides down a few inches. They stand up and chew another piece off. The seeds slide down closer. Soon they get the seeds. They leave the cut stems behind.

SHRIKE

All kinds of mice will store food if they find too much to eat at once. Sometimes you can find these storehouses in hollow logs or dark corners of garages or basements.

You might also find food stored in thornbushes. The shrike, or "butcher bird," is a meat eater. It catches insects and mice. If a shrike finds more than it can eat at once, it hides the rest until later, just like a mouse would. Shrikes keep their food safely stuck on thorns in a thick bush.

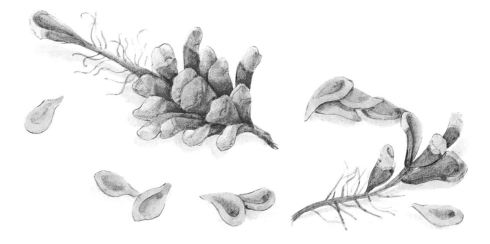

Squirrels leave lots of food clues behind when they eat. Look up. You may see a mushroom tucked high in a tree. A squirrel carried it there and left it to dry. Later he'll store it away in his hole. Look down. You could find a pinecone with all the scales torn off. Squirrels love to eat the pine seeds hidden under each scale. Look where squirrels have been digging. They often bury extra nuts that they gather.

TAWNY OWL PELLET

WORM'S DIRT PILE

BUTTERFLY WINGS

BIRD FEATHERS

Animal's kitchen clues are everywhere. A clump of feathers tells where a bird was eaten by a cat. A pile of butterfly wings or hard beetle wing covers could show where a shrew had an insect breakfast. Little tiny piles of dirt on the ground show where a worm has been working. When they dig, worms eat the dirt to get it out of their way. At night they squirt it out on top of the ground.

An owl doesn't bother to leave the hard parts of its meal behind. If it catches a mouse, it swallows the whole thing. In a few hours, only the mouse's fur, bones, and teeth are left in the owl's stomach. The owl burps. Up come the hard parts in a neat pellet of mouse fur. You can find these owl pellets in the woods, barns, or attics where owls live. They do not smell, and you can pull them apart to see what the owl had for breakfast.

HOW TO TRACK A BEETLE'S FOOD CLUES

If you pull off the bark of an old log you can often find a strange star shape dug into the wood. This is from a borer. This small beetle burrows through the bark to lay its eggs. When the babies hatch, they have plenty of wood to eat in safety under the bark. You can collect the beautiful shapes the babies made as they chewed. Put a piece of clean paper right on top of the star. Rub a pencil point back and forth across the paper, and the shape will show in the rubbing. Try using colored pencils for special stars.

NESTS

If your own room is a mess, you know who will have to clean it up. Lots of animals and birds make nests. Some are messy and some are neat, but it's easy to tell who built them. Can you guess whose homes these are?

You can find birds' nests in the spring by watching birds. When you see one carrying sticks or twigs, follow it. If you see a bird flying to the same place over and over, watch closely. Finding a piece of eggshell does not mean that you are near a nest. Birds carry the empty shells away to make their nests harder to find. When you do find a nest, don't touch it. The parents might leave forever if you do. Wait quietly nearby, and you may see the mother come home. Then you will know for sure whose nest it is.

Some birds lay their eggs right on the ground. These nests are very hard to see, because the eggs are colored just like stones. Killdeers and nighthawks have nests like this. Killdeers like to nest in big yards or fields. If you live in an apartment, you might have a nighthawk nest right on top of your building. They often lay eggs on flat roofs. Once the killdeer or nighthawk babies hatch, there is nothing left to show there ever was a nest.

KILLDEER

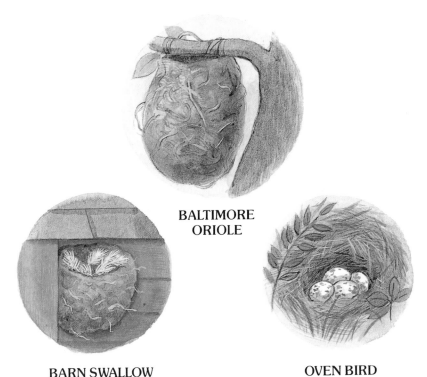

BALTIMORE ORIOLE

BARN SWALLOW

OVEN BIRD

Other birds' nests last long after the birds need them. If you find one in the fall or winter, look at what it was made of and where it was built. These clues can tell you who made the nest. If the nest has lots of mud smoothed over its twigs, it could have been a robin's. They often build muddy nests near people's houses. Barn swallows use nothing but mud to build their nests. Sometimes they stick their nests right on the walls of houses and barns.

A hanging nest high in a tree, made of strips of plant stems and grass, is an oriole's nest. A covered nest made of the same things but built on the ground is an oven-bird's.

A sloppy nest full of surprises is probably a jay's. They love sparkly things. When they build, they use twigs. But they also put in all sorts of other things: Christmas tree tinsel, a key, a scrap of tinfoil, or even a lost earring!

You can make a bird's nest collection. Put the nests in paper or plastic bags with a few mothballs overnight before you bring them indoors. That will kill any insects that might be living in the nests.

Birds are not the only animals who make nests. Rabbits and mice make small, soft nests where they raise their babies. Mouse nests are shaped like balls. They have just one door that they can pull closed to keep their babies safe. Rabbits make their nest in a field or yard. Before their babies are born, they press down a spot in the grass. Then they pull soft fur from their bellies to make that spot warm and cozy.

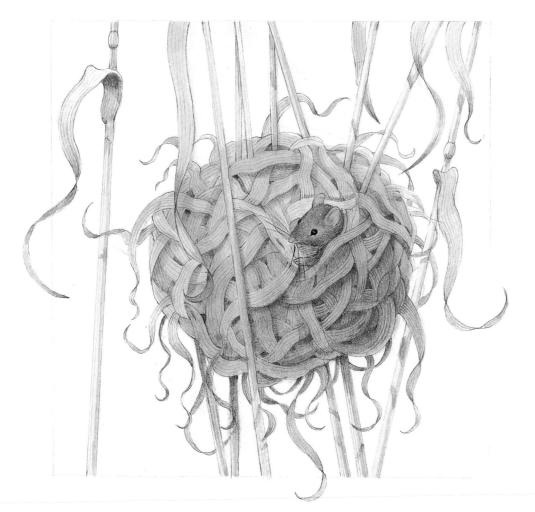

A MOUSE IN ITS NEST

INSIDE A SQUIRREL'S NEST

Squirrels make a winter and a summer nest. Their warm winter nests are usually hidden in hollow trees or attics. Squirrels' summer nests are easy to see. They look like big balls of dead leaves in the tops of trees.

Deer do not make nests, but they do have favorite places to sleep under trees. Their bodies are so big that the plants in these places get squashed. If you find a space where trees grow close together, look for paths worn by sharp deer hooves. Follow the paths and you may come to the deer's home.

When you find one of these animal nests, make a track trap nearby. Be careful not to frighten the animals. Never ruin their homes.

**MUD-DAUBER WASP
AND ITS NEST**

Lots of insects make nests, too. Paper wasps build them from mouthfuls of well-chewed wood. Mud-dauber wasps make nests with mouthfuls of mud. Bees' nests are made of beeswax. The safest time to look at these nests is late on a cool evening, when the insects are asleep and chilled.

One insect nest you can take apart by yourself is a spitbug's. The mother bug blows dozens of bubbles of spit on a plant stem. Then she lays her egg inside and leaves. She knows her baby will be safe and have plenty of food to eat right in its nest.

A gall is a special nest in a plant. The gall insect lays her egg inside a leaf or stem. The plant makes a hard, empty ball around the baby insect. The ball makes a perfect nest. When the insect is ready to get out, it chews a tiny hole through the gall and flies away. If you find a gall without a hole, put it into a jar. You can see what the insect looks like when it comes out. Galls are easy to find in the fall, when leaves drop off the trees.

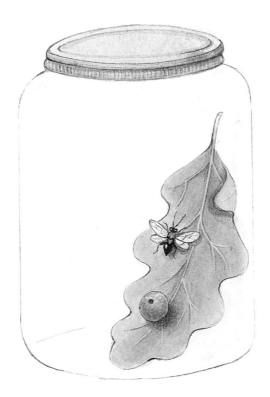

A GALL AND ITS EGG NEST

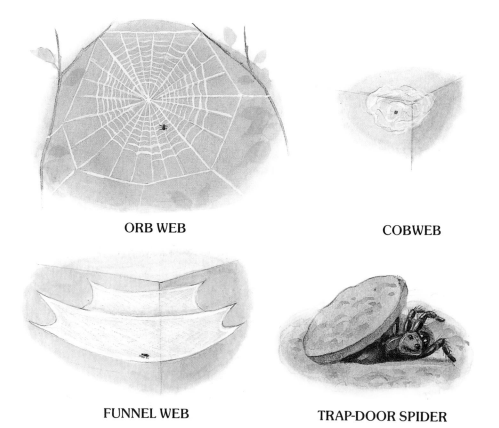

ORB WEB

COBWEB

FUNNEL WEB

TRAP-DOOR SPIDER

Spiders spin their biggest webs in the fall, too. These nests are traps for food as well as homes for the spiders. Like other animals, different kinds of spiders make different kinds of nests. Garden spiders spin round webs where insects are likely to fly into them. Other spiders spin funnel-shaped nests. They hide in the narrow end and rush out to grab insects that land on the wide part. Trap-door spiders live in tunnels under the ground. They make a door that fits tightly. If an insect walks by, the spider pops open the door and jumps out to catch its food. Cobweb spiders spin their webs in loose tangles. You can often see their cobwebs in quiet corners of your house. Even if you don't see the spider, you know what kind is near when you find its web.

HOW TO MAKE AN ANT FARM

Ant babies are safe in their nests underground. You can make an ant farm to bring indoors. All you need is a quart canning jar and lid, a piece of black paper, a square of nylon net or screen, and a skinny olive jar. Put the small jar into the big one and fill in all around it with dirt. Tape black paper around the outside jar. Now you're ready for the ants. Dig as many as you can get from one nest. Get eggs and babies, too. Put them all into the jar with a few crumbs of food. Screw the jar ring down over the net square and set it somewhere out of the sun. When you peek under the black paper in a few days, you can see them at home in their new nest.

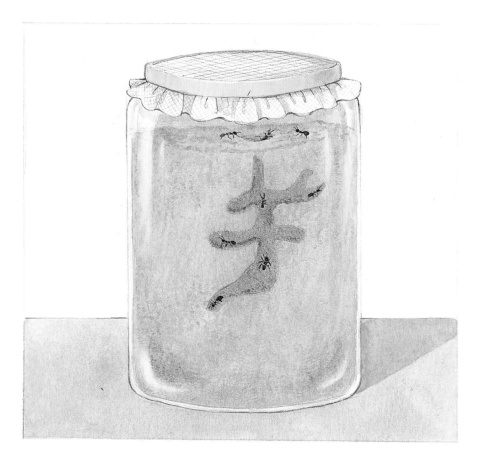

HOW TO COLLECT SPIDERWEBS

You can make a collection of beautiful garden spiderwebs. You need a can of spray paint, two pieces of cardboard, and a pair of scissors. First, chase the spider off its web. Hold a cardboard a few inches behind the web to catch any extra paint. Spray the web until it is all covered and sticky. Carefully press the clean cardboard against the web. Then cut the web loose from the stems that hold it.

TRACKING FUN

Finding an animal by following the clues it leaves behind is called tracking. Indians tracked animals in the woodlands for hundreds of years before Columbus came to America.

You do not have to go to the woods to enjoy tracking. Animal clues are everywhere. You can find tracks and traces in the middle of busy cities and quiet backyards. You can look in nearby parks or zoos for traces of different animals.

Seeing tracks and traces takes practice. On your way to school, keep your eyes moving. Do you see spiderwebs in the bushes? Squirrel nests in the trees? Pigeon feathers on the sidewalk? Wet dog paw prints leading from puddles? You won't see them unless you look carefully.

Play a tracking game with your friends. See who can find the first—or the most—signs of animal life. Work with a partner and see how far you can follow the tracks an animal has left behind.

Try playing hare and hounds. One person is the hare. The hare can run from the hounds in any direction, but must leave tracks and traces all along the way. The clues might be three chalk marks every city block or a crumpled leaf every ten steps along a park path. After the hare gets a head start, the hounds begin following the tracks. The hound who finds the hare first wins. In this game, everybody gets a prize: they all learn more about tracking.

If you are tracking wild animals in a park or in the country, leave your friends, your dog, and your radio at home. To see wild animals, you need to be very quiet. You need to move slowly. And you need to keep your mind on traces. That is very hard to do with more than one friend.

When you find a nest or a place where there are lots of different animal traces, you might want to "hide and peek." To see the shiest animals, you have to hide in a blind. A big cardboard box with peep holes cut into it makes a good blind. You do have to be quiet in a blind, but you can move around as you wait to see animals.

If you can sit very still for half an hour outdoors, animals seem to forget that you are there. They will come out of hiding and play or eat while you watch. Put peanut butter or seed bait down before you start to be still, and animals will come near you to eat. But if you make a noise or move quickly, they will all hurry back to their hiding places again.

Our world is full of animals. The wild ones aren't easy to see, and they like it that way. Now you know how to read many of the tracks and traces they leave behind. As you practice your tracking skills, you will get to know animals that most people never even see.

GLOSSARY

body feathers. Smooth feathers that cover down

borer. An insect that burrows through wood just under the bark of a tree

claw. A sharp, pointed toenail

clue. Anything that helps to solve a mystery

down. Fluffy feathers that lie next to a bird's skin

ferret. A small, weasellike animal

gall. A hollow swelling made by a plant around an insect egg

hoof. A thick toenail grown by animals that walk on the tips of their toes

odor. A smell

owl pellet. The tight clump of fur, teeth, and bones that owls burp up a few hours after eating

path. A place where the ground and plants have been pressed flat by many footsteps

pellet. A small, tidy clump

print. The mark left by a damp or dirty paw

scales. Thin, flat plates that stiffen the skin of many animals and birds

scent. A smell that is not strong

shaft. The stiff strip down the middle of a feather

shed. To leave old fur, skin, or feathers behind

shedding. Dropping old, worn fur or skin to make room for a new covering

shrike. A large gray or brownish bird with a hooked bill

trace. A very small clue left by something

track. The shape of a foot or paw pressed into soft ground

tracking. Following an animal you cannot see by finding the clues it left behind

urine. Watery body waste

ANSWERS TO TRACKING PUZZLES

Page 6
Can you tell which animals left these traces?

LONG-EARED OWL: PELLET

BIRD: FEATHERS

DEER: TRACKS

Page 8
Can you guess from these clues who was here?

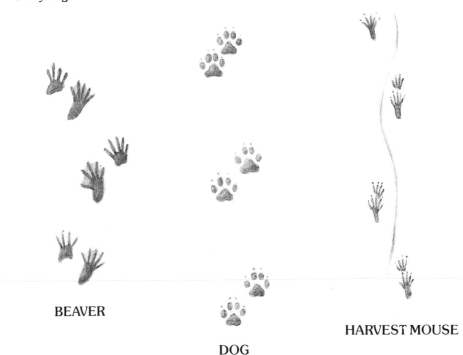

BEAVER

DOG

HARVEST MOUSE

Page 10
Can you tell these animal tracks apart?

OPOSSUM

RACCOON

Page 10
Which animal made which track?

MOOSE

WHITE-TAIL DEER

Page 13
Can you guess who left behind these "dirty clothes"?

ORANGE SULPHUR BUTTERFLY:
WING

LOCUST: SHELL

FOX: FUR ON BARBED WIRE

Page 22
Which animals left these clues behind when they finished eating?

SQUIRREL: GNAWED PINECONES

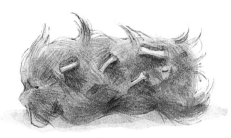

OWL: PELLET

MOOSE: GNAWED NUTSHELLS

46

Pages 28–29
Can you guess whose homes these are?

WEAVERBIRD

BEAVER

REED WARBLER

INDEX